T5-AGA-417

DELINQUENCY PRONENESS: A COMPARISON OF DELINQUENT TENDENCIES IN MINORS UNDER COURT SUPERVISION
PHYLLIS LEVINE

San Francisco, California
1978

BRESCIA COLLEGE
LIBRARY

41718

Published By

R & E RESEARCH ASSOCIATES, INC.
4848 Mission Street
San Francisco, California 94112

Publishers
Robert D. Reed and Adam S. Eterovich

Library of Congress Card Catalog Number
77-90356

I.S.B.N.
0-88247-516-9

Copyright 1978
By
Phyllis Levine

TABLE OF CONTENTS

APPENDICES

iv

LIST OF TABLES

CHAPTER I

INTRODUCTION

The Los Angeles County Juvenile Court supervises minors under three sections of the Welfare and Institutions Code. Section 600 refers to minors who are without proper parental care or control, minors who are victims of neglect or abuse. Section 601 refers to the incorrigible minors, school truants and runaway juveniles. Under this section are the minors (under age 18) who, had they been adults, would not be guilty of any code violations; these offenses are commonly called the "status crimes". Section 602 refers to minors who have violated Penal Code sections, ranging from shoplifting to murder. Included in this group, however, are minors who have violated an order imposed upon them in prior 601 proceedings. For example, a truant minor may violate a court order to attend school regularly and, therefore, be in violation of Section 602. He or she then becomes as "delinquent" as, and subject to, the same conditions as a minor who has committed murder.

Current trends in Los Angeles County prohibit intermixing of these minors in detention facilities. However, this separation ends when the Court orders a minor returned to his own home and, therefore, to the non-court supervised neighborhood as well, or when placement in a children's institution is ordered. In these institutions, no effort is made to keep minors separate based on their court status. These placement facilities house minors in a variety of ways, including age, problem, social needs,

1

or special interests, even including where space is available when the minor enters the facility. None of these takes court status into account. Yet, the detention centers and the courts have been adamant in their orders of separation.

In 1968, supervision of minors under Section 600 was transferred from the Probation Department to the Department of Public Social Services, the assumption being that these minors are not delinquents and need social work services rather than punitive measures. It was felt that Probation Officers' training was on a penal scale and not appropriate for neglected children. In early 1975, the Los Angeles County Board of Supervisors strongly urged the separation of Section 601 and 602 minors, feeling that the "hard core" 602 delinquents were adversely affection the lesser violators.

When minors are detained, the Section 600 minors go to MacLaren Hall, and the 601's and 602's go to Central Juvenile Hall or Los Padrinos Hall. Here they are housed separately. The girls detained under Section 602 are kept separately at Los Padrinos Hall. The boys under this section are at Central Juvenile Hall as well. Minors detained under Section 601 are at Central Juvenile Hall, apart from the 602's boys and girls kept in separate sides of the building. However, if the Court recommends out-of-home placement, these minors often go to the institutions contracting with Los Angeles County, which have populations that are mixed and where the minors are treated according to their needs, rather than their "records."

It should be noted that serious offenders and hard core violators usually are sent to Probation camps or the California Youth Authority, and are not mixed during times of detention in the Juvenile Halls. For the purposes of this study, the latter are not included.

Focus of the Study

This study, limited by confidentiality regulations of the Los Angeles County Probation and Public Social Services Departments, the institutions involved and the high school tested, focuses on minors who have come to the attention of the Juvenile Court for any of the reasons covered under Sections 600, 601 and 602 of the Welfare and Institutions Code. Only minors going through the detention process were tested prior to placement, while minors tested in two placement institutions, Pacific Lodge for Boys and Maryvale for girls, were there for all the reasons described in the Welfare and Institutions Code, as well as for problems resulting from poor home environments not coming to the attention of the court. These are the so-called "voluntary placement" minors, whose parents have chosen placement as an alternative to unsatisfactory home conditions. Because of the confidential nature of the records kept by the various institutions, only age and sex were asked as identifying information. It was possible to tell by the location what code section the detained minors came under; however, for those minors in the two institutions and those in the high school, it was not possible to ask this information. Therefore, for purposes of this study, we will look only at the delinquency of detained minors, as opposed to those in a County placement and will compare these minors with high school students.

3

The mixture of delinquent and non-delinquent minors after the court proceedings may show an overall increase in proneness from that of the minors, considered non-delinquent, at MacLaren Hall. This could mean mixture tends to increase delinquency in the non-delinquent minor. On the other hand a decrease in delinquency proneness after placement could indicate success in the treatment plan or possible peer group pressure toward non-delinquent behavior. The focus on these three types of minors, therefore, has several purposes.

Purpose of the Study

The purpose of this study is to determine to what extent, if any, 600, 601 and 602 minors exhibit delinquent tendencies and how they differ from each other and other minors in the community. It is not possible to isolate these minors other than in the detention facilities, and, therefore, it is important to determine the extent of delinquent behavior before and after placement. If there is an increase in delinquent proneness on the part of the 600 and 601 minors after placement, the entire Juvenile Justice and protection system as it now exists must be altered. However, it is felt that in a significant number of cases, the behavior defined as delinquent exists in all three groups prior to court action. This study intends to test whether these minors show similarities in delinquent proneness. A control group from a high school felt to have a similar ethnic composition with court minors was selected.

Most of the literature on delinquency indicates a positive correlation between delinquent behavior and deprivation (both physical and emotional).

4

Section 600, by definition, includes these victims, and, therefore, it is reasonable to assume the Section 600 minors will score high on delinquent proneness.

Need for the Study

Because of the rising crisis in the Juvenile Court system and the need to find, if not a solution to juvenile crime, at least a more effective way of dealing with it, a study of minors under Court supervision is essential. To help these minors adapt to adult society, we need to know which environments are detrimental or helpful to their development. This study is a first step to this type of research--to find out how to handle juveniles before, during and after intervention of the Court in a manner which will prevent further delinquent behavior or peer group pressure into delinquent behavior. Based on the results of this study, some recommendations can be made regarding confinement and treatment of troubled youth.

Null Hypothesis

Minors entering the Juvenile Court system under Sections 600, 601 and 602 of the Welfare and Institutions Code, show no significant differences in delinquent tendencies.

Research Hypothesis

Minors entering the Juvenile Court system under Sections 600, 601 and 602 show increasing delinquent tendencies; Section 600 minors show lower delinquent tendencies that 601's, and 602's score highest in delinquency.

Testing

The KD Proneness Scale is to be administered to: (1) newly detained minors at MacLaren Hall; (2) detained minors at Central Juvenile Hall and Los Padrinos Hall; (3) minors currently placed at two of the institutions contracting with Los Angeles County to care for minors, Pacific Lodge for boys and Maryvale for girls; and (4) students at a metropolitan high school which has a good ethnic mixture and a similar socio-economic level to minors under court supervision. This is a 20 to 45 minute (depending on literacy level) multiple choice test designed to measure delinquency proneness. It will be anonymous, asking only age and sex.

Assumptions

It is expected that all three categories of minors will have similar scores on the test. The presumed cause of delinquency is the situational aspects of Section 600, therefore, most minors coming within the provisions of Section 600 have suffered the deprivations usually associated with delinquency. It is expected that the treatment model used could be essentially the same for all three, and this is the premise upon which the current treatment facilities are operating. Accepting this assumption, should minors currently at Maryvale and Pacific Lodge score better on the test, we can hope the treatment offered at these institutions has been beneficial.

Organization of the Study

The remainder of this study is organized as follows:

(1) Chapter II presents a review of the literature on delinquency causation and on the social problems leading to court intervention.

6

(2) Chapter III deals with the methodology, testing procedures and data analysis.

(3) Chapter IV is the presentation of data and analysis.

(4) Chapter V deals with interpretation of the data and makes some recommendations for further study.

CHAPTER II

REVIEW OF THE LITERATURE

Webster defines delinquent as "offending by neglect or violation of duty or of law." Further research turns up many and varied definitions of the term and its use in describing the behavior of minors. In addition to its law violation concept, delinquency in California, as described in Section 601 of the Welfare and Institutions Code, includes such behaviors as truancy, curfew violation and runaway. These "status crimes" are deemed illegal only when committed by a minor. Further:

> In defining Juvenile Delinquency, laws are of little use. Usually laws are specific only in relation to serious adult offenses such as murder, assault. . .etc. Children are delinquent if they are found guilty in court of breaching any of the federal, state or local laws designed to control adult behavior. Delinquency statistics, however, indicate that these serious offenses account for only a small proportion of the delinquencies of children. Most of the behavior that gets a child into trouble with the police and courts comes under a much less definite part of the law on juvenile delinquency. Examples are easy to find. The Illinois law defines as delinquent a child who is incorrigible or who is growing up in idleness, one who wanders about the streets in the night time without being on any lawful business or one who is guilty of indecent or lascivious conduct. Laws in some other states are still more vague. New Mexico rests its definition on the word "habitual." A delinquent child is one who by habitually refusing to obey the reasonable and lawful commands of his parents or other persons of lawful authority, is deemed to be habitually wayward, or who so deports himself as to injure or endanger the morals, health, or welfare of himself or others. In these laws, there is no definition of such words or phrases as incorrigible, habitual, indecent conduct or in the nighttime. (Caven, 1961, 243)

The Task Force Report: Juvenile Delinquency and Youth Crime (1967), in discussing status offenses, found vague terminology, easily manipulated definitions and moral judgments. Such terminology as "growing up in idleness," engaging in "immoral conduct" and "in danger of leading an immoral life," when used with the informality of the Juvenile Court, provide the Judge power to rule on the behavior and morals of the minors and their parents.

The California Welfare and Institutions Code defines the status offense violator in Section 601 of the Code:

> Any person under the age of 18 years who persistently or habitually refuses to obey the reasonable and proper orders or directions of his parents, guardian, custodian or school authorities, or who is beyond the control of such person, or any person who is a habitual truant from school within the meaning of any law of this state, or who from any cause is in danger of leading an idle dissolute, lewd or immoral life, is within the jurisdiction of the juvenile court which may adjudge such person to be a ward of the court.

These are the so-called "status crimes"--crimes which would not be so defined if committed by an adult. While varying in different jurisdictions, this behavior can include use of vile language, smoking, drinking or even "hanging around." Paul Tappan, quoted by Goldstein, Freud and Solnit, observes, "to many they appear to describe the normal behavior of the little-inhibited and non-neurotic child." At one time or another, we presume the majority of our children violate this section.

Section 602 of the Code States:

> Any person who is under the age of 18 years when he violates any law of this state, or of the United States or any ordinance of any city or county of this state defining crime, or who, after having been found by the Juvenile Court to be a person described by Section 601, fails to obey any lawful order of the Juvenile Court, is within the jurisdiction of the Juvenile Court which may adjudge such person to be a Ward of the Court.

9

These are the Penal Code violators -- the "true delinquents" who have committed crimes.

Another element of the Juvenile Court must be mentioned. This is the case of the non-delinquent minors placed in the Custody of the Court for protection from abuse or neglect by their parents or the minors who have no parents or guardians to provide for their care. These children are described in California under Section 600 of the Welfare and Institutions Code:

> Section 600. PERSONS WITHIN JURISDICTION OF THE COURT. Any person under the age of 18 years who comes within any of the following descriptions is within the jurisdiction of the Juvenile Court. (a) who is in need of proper and effective parental care or control and has no parent or guardian, or has no parent or guardian willing to exercise or capable of exercising such care or control, or has no parent or guardian actually exercising such care or control.
> (b) who is destitute, or who is not provided with the necessities of life, or who is not provided with a home or suitable place of abode.
> (c) who is physically dangerous to the public because of a mental or physical deficiency, disorder, or abnormality.
> (d) whose home is an unfit place for him by reason of neglect, cruelty, depravity, or physical abuse of either of his parents or of his guardian or other person in whose custody or care he is.

Minors going to court under these circumstances have been abused or exploited by their families, subjected to unsafe supervision, dangerous and filthy surroundings, been denied the necessities of life and health due to their parents' disabilities or negligence. Many of these children are the victims of ineffective or rejecting parents. In particular, minors of emotionally disturbed parents often live a chaotic existence with unpredictable, inconsistent parental guidance.

The Welfare and Institutions Code further addresses the problem of detention:

> Section 506. SEGREGATION OF DEPENDENTS AND DELIN-
> QUENTS. No person taken into custody solely upon the ground
> that he is a person described in Section 600 or adjudged to be
> such and made a Dependent Child of the Juvenile Court pursuant
> to this chapter solely upon that ground shall, in any detention
> under this chapter, be brought into direct contact or personal
> association with any person described by Section 601 or Section
> 602, or who has been made a Ward of the Juvenile Court on
> either such ground.
> Separate segregated facilities for such persons alleged to
> be within the description of Section 600, or persons adjudged to
> be such and made Dependent Children of the Court pursuant to
> this chapter solely upon that ground shall be provided by the
> Board of Supervisors. Such separate, segregated facilities
> may be provided in the Juvenile Hall or elsewhere.

This paper proposes that minors, specifically those between ages 12 and 17, coming into the Los Angeles County Juvenile Justice System under Sections 600, 601 and 602, Welfare and Institutions Code, have similar delinquent tendencies due to the similarity of environmental hardships. Many studies have been made on delinquency causation, and causal elements are often the elements defined in Section 600: parents unable or unwilling to provide a suitable home, unable or unwilling to provide appropriate supervision, parents with deviant behavior resulting in child endangering and physical and mental handicaps rendering the individual minor a danger to himself or others.

Crime and Juvenile Delinquency Statistics

FBI statistics show a 148% increase in the index crimes reported between 1960 and 1969; at the same time, the population increase was 13%

and the total crime rate increase was 120%. The juvenile crime statistics for the same period reveal the volume of arrest of persons under 18 years of age, for all offenses except traffic, increased four times the percentage rate of increase in the population. The number of minors ages ten through 17 in the population increased 27%, and arrest rates for those under 18 years doubled. In regard to Index Crimes, the increase is 90%, with a 148% increase for violent crimes and an 85% increase in property offenses. The total population between ages ten and 17 is equal to 16% of the whole population. Yet, of the Index Crimes solved during this period, persons under age 18 accounted for 32%. The rate is still higher when we consider that in many self-tests (usually administered anonymously and through questionaire) as many as 90% of the individuals admit to having committed acts which, had they been apprehended, would have resulted in arrest. In California, juvenile arrests make up one-third of the arrests. In Los Angeles County, statistics through Fall of 1975 show a 13% increase in juvenile offenses over the 1974 figures. Of the 24,534 juveniles referred to the Los Angeles County Probation Department for the period from July, 1974 to June, 1975, 2,296 were for violations of Section 601 and 22,166 for violations of Section 602. Current figures kept by the Los Angeles County Sheriff's Department and Los Angeles Police Department, indicate over 400 juvenile gangs known to be active in the county. We may also assume that there exists more juvenile organizations of a more or less delinquent nature that have not yet been identified. Since April 1, 1969, when Dependency matters, Section 600, were separated from other juvenile programs, of the approximate 29,000 minors who come via petition filings, to the attention of the Los Angeles County Juvenile Court System annually, 15% come under this Section of the Welfare and Institutions Code, alleging they have been the victims of parental abuse or neglect necessitating court intervention. Since these figures are often combined, "600" minors with the so-called delinquency minors, there exists somewhat of a skew in the statistics in some instances. However, the fact remains that with 114,200 juvenile arrests in Los Angeles County in 1974, many for status offenses and minor crimes, juvenile involvement in the court system is rising. In addition to this, 30,000 children per year receive services relating to juvenile problems through the Welfare Department.

History of the Juvenile Court

The provision for differential treatment of juveniles goes as far back as the Code of Hammurabi in 2270 B.C. when specific punishments were used for children who disowned their parents or ran away from home. The early Hebrews divided childhood into three categories--infant, prepubescent and adolescent--and increased severity of punishment with age increase. Old English Law provided lesser punishment for those under age.

The Task Force Report (1967) summarized the history of the Juvenile Court in the United States. The Parens Patriae philosophy of feudal England, when the Chancery Court exercised protective jurisdiction over all children for the King ("Pater Patriae"), was used primarily to protect property rights of minors. When the English system came to the United States, this was extended to include minors in danger of personal injury as well, and became the basis of the Juvenile Court protection system in the United States; however, the Chancery Court dealt only with neglected and dependent children, not those accused of criminal action. The English Common Law imposed a duty on parents to provide support, supervision and care of their children. The present day delinquency courts have a less clear history. One concept of delinquency comes from the Common Law, which presumed a child under age seven was not capable of intent; from seven to 14 he could be evaluated regarding intent. The existence of these attitudes presupposes the existence of juvenile law violations. Other theorists, including the Children's Bureau, emphasize the unique quality of the Juvenile Court in the United States and deny its growth from Chancery Courts.

The 19th Century reform movement brought new concerns with the mounting truancy and delinquency problems, and emphasis shifted to rescuing children from the "bad" influences of such things as tobacco, alcohol and pornography. The recognition of the greater vulnerability of youth and the facility of their "rehabilitation" led to the separation of proceedings from adult courts, and separate institutions were formulated.

In 1825, the House of Refuge in New York City was founded. Here children were separated from adult offenders and given "correctional" treatment rather than punishment. Later came state reform and industrial schools, the first established in Massachusetts in 1847. These institutions were "aimed at teaching youths discipline and an honest trade and instilling dedication to advancement through hard work." (Task Force Report,

14

1967, p. 3) In 1880, Probation first was established as an alternative to incarceration, reflecting the increase in social science techniques of treatment and supervision as preventative measures.

According to the Report, "Awareness of the brutality of incarcerating children with adult criminals led to efforts to separate them before and during trial as well." (Task Force Report, 1967, p. 3) In 1861, the Mayor of Chicago was authorized to appoint a commissioner to hear minor charges against teenage boys; in 1867, judges assumed this role. Two years later, in Massachusetts, court agents were provided for minors for who reform school might be prescribed; further, the agent was to find homes and provide home visits (as is done today by Los Angeles County Deputy Probation Officers and Children's Services Workers). In Boxton (Suffolk County), separate hearings were authorized, with appropriate representation of the "children's interests." New York followed suit in 1872, and Rhode Island in 1892.

The "wayward child" concept first arose in 1899, when Illinois passed the Juvenile Court Act creating a state-wide court for minors. This brought dependent, neglected and delinquent children (including "incorrigibles and children threatened by immoral associations" as well as criminallaw violators) together under the same jurisdiction. Informal hearings, non-public and confidential, were held apart from adults. By 1925, all but two states had Juvenile Courts, and today all states and Washington D.C. have such facilities.

Haskell and Yablonsky (1974) cite a list of juvenile court characteristics considered essential by the Children's Bureau in 1920:

> (1) Separate hearings for children; (2) Informal or Chancery procedure; (3) Regular Probation service; (4) Separate detention for children; (5) Special court and probation records; (6) Provision for mental and physical examination.

According to Paul Lerman:

> One of the most "progressive" juvenile court laws in the country was initially enacted with restrictions on mixing, but this was soon amended to permit the change to be merely semantic, not substantive. (1973, p. 260)

At present, seven states have established procedures to distinguish criminal and non-criminal acts in the Juvenile Court (California, New York, Illinois, Kansas, Colorado, Oklahoma, Vermont). New York refers to these children as PINS (Persons in Need of Supervision) and provides separate adjudication without alleging delinquency. However, both types of children, PINS and crime violators, are locked up in the same detention facilities and reform schools.

In Los Angeles County, in recent months, greater emphasis has been placed on the dangers of mixture and social interaction between the three types of court-supervised minors: the "600's" (neglected and abused), the "601's" (pre-delinquent and status offenders), and the "602's" (criminal law violators). Initially, the separation of 600's was implemented by transfer of their supervision from the Probation Department to the Department of Public Social Services; later refusal to allow their detention in the same facilities as other minors, and a separation of court locations and staff allowed for complete segregation. Next the Probation Department provided separate detention of 601's, keeping them away from the more ser-

ious violators. At present, these efforts have resulted in initial separation;

however, when these minors leave the detention center, they often go to in-

stitutions or treatment centers for behavioral and emotional difficulties.

In these institutions, minors are intermixed, usually on the basis of sex,

age, interest or type of problem. At this point, the three types of minors

are again involved in social interaction.

Major Causation Studies

A review of the literature on delinquency shows many theories--of

causation and non-causation.

Early work, from the 1920's to the 1950's, concentrated on the ob-

vious causative factors of poverty, broken homes, gang membership, ab-

sense of father figures and many equally broad elements. As more sophis-

ticated studies have been done, the causative elements have changed some-

what. The 1950 White House Conference on Children and Youth recom-

mended that work with delinquents and non-delinquents be based on an un-

derstanding of motivation and social situations. Because no single answer

exists for delinquency prevention, no single approach can be used.

Albert Cohen (1925) deals with theories on social class variables. He

concerns himself primarily with lower class delinquency. He found lower

class boys were lacking in self esteem and had a high degree of status frus-

tration because of class position.

In Delinquent Boys: The Culture of the Gang (1955), Cohen describes

the delinquent subculture as non-utilitarian, malicious and negativistic;

the delinquent subculture turns the cultures and norms of the society upside down. A conspicuous element in delinquency for Cohen is intolerance of restraint except as applied by the peer group itself. He disagrees with the social disorganization theory as it doesn't answer the questions of the origin of impulse. Finally, Cohen does allow that as Dr. Kvaraceus' study of the Passaic Children's Bureau in 1945 showed, the overwhelming majority subculture is more common in the working class, says Cohen, and the "position of the family determines the experiences and problems members of the family will encounter in dealings with the outside world." (1955)

Clifford Shaw and Henry McKay, starting in 1929, in Chicago, studied Juvenile Courts and concluded:

> There is a marked variation in delinquency rates between different areas of Chicago; rates of delinquency and adult crime vary inversely with distance from city center; truancy, delinquency and crime rates are positively correlated; high crime rates are found in areas of physical deterioration; crime rates remain stable over time especially in high crime areas, despite changes in population; recidivism varies directly with the delinquency rate. (Shaw and McKay, 1942)

They concluded that the community is at the root of delinquency.

The Cambridge Sommerville Study of the 1950's rated neighborhoods in which subjects lived according to community organization, dilapidation and prevalence of gangs. Four types of environment were found: (1) cohesive; (2) quarrelsome but affectionate; (3) quarrelsome and neglecting; and (4) broken homes. It was found that the quarrelsome neglecting homes had the highest probability of producing criminal behavior. The study analyzes five father types: (1) passive; (2) warm and affectionate; (3) ne-

18

glecting, rejecting; (4) cruel; (5) absent. The neglecting, rejecting father was found to be more productive of delinquent offspring (1951).

The Gluecks' studies, starting in 1950, found five characteristics of delinquents' homes: (1) . . . homes in which the relationship between the parents is not cohesive and "good"; (2) . . . homes in which discipline is lax, in which the parents use physical punishment, and in which the parents less often use reasoning as a method of control; (3) They come from parents who themselves have criminal records; (4) They have a lower average intelligence; (5) They have feelings of being unloved and rejected. This analysis came from a study in which they found five factors influencing delinquency: father's discipline; mother's discipline; family cohesiveness; mother's affection; father's affection. (Glueck and Glueck, 1950) According to the Gluecks, parents of delinquents have a higher incidence of criminality, mental retardation, emotional disturbances, drunkenness and serious physical ailments than the non-delinquent control group they used in their study. Their studies, beginning in 1940, compared 500 delinquents and 500 non-delinquent boys, all from underprivileged neighborhoods, and determined characteristics of family members. They found in many cases the "under the roof" cultural differences were significant while poverty, poor health, ethnic and neighborhood characteristics were similar. The Gluecks found mental backwardness in one of seven non-delinquent families, but one in four in delinquent families. One-fourth of the families of delinquents and one-fifth of non-delinquents had severe emotional disturbance, sex inversions, emotional inside of the delinquent's family had a high-

19

er incidence of emotional disturbance (four to two). Almost one-half of the delinquents had mothers with alcoholic problems, compared with one-third of the non-delinquents.

> It would seem obvious that fathers and mothers who them-
> selves had been reared in an atmosphere of poverty combined
> with intellectual and educational inferiority, physical and men-
> tal disease, alcoholism and criminalism would not be likely to
> bring to the task of child rearing the intelligence, the solid mo-
> ral standards, the ethical and religious ideals, and the peace of
> mind so indispensable to the wholesome emotional and intellec-
> tual rearing of youngsters especially in the highly competitive,
> predatory and generally exciting environment of the under pri-
> vileged urban areas. (Glueck and Glueck, 1950, p. 42)

Additional differences were found in work habits of fathers of delinquents, in income management (delinquents' families were more "slipshod"),
and in amount of family pride, it being less common in delinquents' families.
Further, the Gluecks concluded, the conduct standards in the delinquents'
homes were less harmonious and supervision was more lax.

> Certainly material neglect and careless oversight of children
> are generally recognized as major sources of maladaptation
> and delinquency, and clearly the mothers of the delinquent
> boys as a group were far more remiss in the care of their
> children than were the mothers of the non-delinquents. (Glueck
> and Glueck, 1950, p. 52)

Cultural anthropologist Walter Miller, in 1958-59, defined lower class
delinquency as not deviant except from a middle class view. He found delinquency a part of lower class culture and functional in helping the youth prepare for adult life in that social class. He further discussed the female
based household and lack of father figure of the lower class, resulting in
the need for boys to practice assertion of their masculinity. Miller put
most emphasis on the family.

20

Cloward and Ohlin's studies (1960) deal with goals and means of achieving them. Using the community setting, they found that the way legitimate and illegitimate means are integrated into the community will determine the way the delinquent achieves them. This "opportunity theory" states in essence that the lack of opportunity for legitimate means and the opportunity for use of illegitimate means will result in delinquent behavior.

Albert Cohen, in a PhD Thesis, Harvard Univesity, 1951, cites a study in which 170 distinct conditions conducive to child misconduct were found. Walter B. Miller concluded that the perception of the delinquent act by the individual himself determines motivation, and to understand motivation, the cultural forces should be studied.

Most would agree that, as Malcolm Klein stated, it is "not the family per se which is important, but factors of the family: broken homes, working mothers, criminal experiences, supervision, affection, modes of discipline." (Klein, 1971, p. 36). Family factors, though important, are combined with many other factors.

Studies of Living Styles

It becomes apparent that the miscellaneous combinations of individual and social backgrounds of the pre-delinquent and the delinquent or the neglected child are similar. The home problems present and described in Section 600 of the California Welfare and Institutions Code, are broad definitions of the causality factors of "broken" homes, family dis-unity, lack of parental figues, lack of supervision, excessive alcohol and drug use at home.

A-1718

Gene Kassebaum quotes the President's <u>Crime Commission Report</u>

describing a common living situation among delinquent children:

> What the inner city child calls home is often a set
> of rooms shared by a shifting group of relatives and ac-
> quaintances--furniture shabby and sparse, many children
> in one bed, plumbing failing, plaster falling, roaches in the
> corners and sometimes rats, hallways dark or dimly lighted,
> stairways littered, air dank and foul. Inadequate unsanitary
> facilities complicate keeping clean. Disrepair discourages
> neatness. Insufficient heating, multiple use of bathrooms
> and kitchens, crowded sleeping arrangements spread and
> multiply respiratory infections and communicable diseases.
> Rickety, shadowy stairways and bad electrical connections
> take their accidental toll. Rat bites are not infrequent and
> sometimes, especially for infants, fatal. Care of one's own
> and respect for others' possessions can hardly be inculcated
> in such surroundings. More important, home has little
> holding power for the child--it is not physically pleasant
> or attractive; it is not a place to bring his friends; it is
> not even very much the reassuring gathering place of his
> own family. The loss of parental control and diminishing
> adult supervision that occur so early in the slum child's
> life must thus be laid at least partly at the door of his home.
> (Kassebaum, 1974, p. 19).

These living standards are described in Section 600 of the <u>Welfare</u>

<u>and Institutions Code</u>. From this we must assume that the children from

the neglecting homes have been subjected to these situations, as well as

others connected with delinquency causation factors. The <u>Task Force</u>

<u>Report</u> found the "average delinquent to be 15 or 16, from a large family,

possibly with multiple fathers, that is female centered, receiving "leniency,

sternness, affection, perhaps indifference, in erratic and unpredictable

succession. " (1967)

Several writings have made reference to selective enforcement of the

juvenile laws. Haskel and Yablonsky state:

The legal status of the "delinquent" tends to depent more on the attitudes of the parents, the police, the community and the juvenile courts than on any specific illegal behavior of the child. (Haskell and Yablonsky, 1974, p. 3)

They find that parental attitudes are influential, particularly when a choice of defining the minor as incorrigible or disobedient. One parent may ask for court action while another will feel the same behavior is normal and acceptable.

Howard James (1969) cites four variables determining the outcome of a minor's involvement with law enforcement: (1) the agency or individual that first becomes concerned; (2) the "whims and prejudices" of the judge; (3) the social and economic standing of the family; (4) the community resources available. Police intervention combined with disinterested family, pushes the minor toward delinquency. A neighbor noticing a problem may involve the child with the Welfare Department. The school may recommend institutional treatment. Kassebaum (1974) iterates that the difference between neglect and dependency seems to be whether the child has a parent or guardian providing supervision, even if neglectful, or if there is no one legally responsible for him. In the former, the court has more judgment as to the propriety of taking custody; in the latter, the child is detained. Again the availability of resources is an issue. However, a minor accused of violating one of the status crimes, particularly incorrigibility, usually has an ongoing conflict at home. For this reason, he, whose law violation is considered minor, is subjected to greater punishment and longer confinement than a more serious offender because he has no resources, i.e., home, available for him.

Paul Lerman in Delinquents Without Crime (1973), finds juvenile status offenders "tend to have more family troubles and may actually have greater difficulty in meeting the criteria for release (from detention facilities) than their delinquent peers." (Lerman, 1973) William Kvaraceus (1959) feels a child with two parents to "back him up" has a better chance of getting a break in court. With two parents helping, he may appear as a problem child who could be referred to a clinic or other professional service for help. However, if the home lacks middle class, two-parent cultural elements, the child has a better chance of ending up in an institution. The delinquent act in the context of the lower class family is prosecuted, while the same act in the middle class is treated or often considered normal behavior.

Paul Lerman, cited in Children and their Caretakers (Danzin, 1973) reports that juvenile status offenders, by the nature of their offense, tend to have more family troubles than their delinquent counterparts. This results in harsher treatment and longer time spent in institutions designed for the true delinquent. According to Lerman, this procedure not only creates undue punishment for some, but undermines any concept of justice for juvenile law violators. Richette (1970) in The Throwaway Children, notes instances where affluent delinquent gang members are seen as good children who have gone bad. They are allowed to buy their way out of trouble (through more competent or skilled attorneys or through availability of corrective resources in their communities). Thus, the class and status

24

systems for the juvenile court tend to be prejudicial in two areas:
incorrigible "turned in" by his family after a family fight; the affl
delinquent is excused and, therefore, not helped because of his family's
status.

Mary Gillespie of Long Beach (California) Legal Aid, in an address
before the Los Angeles County Public Social Services Commission (1974)
noted that most juvenile cases get into court because the parents are poor.
Alicia Escalante, Welfare Rights Organization Officer, at the same hearings, stated that people on welfare are more vulnerable by the nature of
their circumstances. The Task Force Report, The Challenge of Crime
in a Free Society (1967), notes "Poverty and racial discrimination, bad
housing. . .the enormous gap between American ideals and American
achievements" are recognized as causatives.

Donald Brieland in Contemporary Social Work, states:

> Conditions within the neighborhood and community are the
> primary cause of many problems. National issues and influences
> and the resultant neglect of the family as a unit of attention and
> concern in public social policy are also important. (Brieland,
> 1975, p. 269)

Brieland continues to delineate some of the problems bringing children to
the attention of the social agencies: poorly functioning family life due to
poverty, causing denial of adequate food, clothing and care, with drab
neighborhoods without necessary services to insure adequate development;
migrant labor conditions, allowing children to be used as laborers to
support the family, thereby neglecting their education; impersonal care
often provided by non-parents or institutions where the children may remain

25

.n the absence of effective or available parents; running away of teenagers who feel alienated from their families or from schools or their community, many trying to escape conflict with family members or with their parents way of life, or attempting to find individuality or adventure in a new environment. Brieland describes the experience of running away as, "one of loneliness, untreated health problems, precipitous experimentation with sex, harmful use of drugs and disillusionment." (Brieland, 1975, p. 269)

William C. Kvaraceus finds:

. . .more delinquents as children of lower status have been confronted by many more problems of living, have undergone more frustrations, and have been given less help in their growth and development toward dominant middle class virtues than the children of higher status. (Kvaraceus, 1954, p. 36)

Further:

Atypical homes, lack of family cohesiveness, school failure, truancy and unsupervised play are more peculiar to the backgrounds of delinquents than non-delinquents. (Kvaraceus, 1954, p. 40)

Paul Lerman states:

Certain young people in American society are more likely to have troubles with adults: girls, poor youth, rural migrants to the city, underachievers, and the less sophisticated. Historically, a community's more disadvantaged children are most likely to have their troubles defined as delinquency. In the 1830's, the kids of Irish immigrants were over-represented in the nation's juvenile correctional institutions. In the 1970's, the black slum kids are disproportionately dealt with as delinquents for experiencing problems in growing up. (Lerman, 1973)

Barbara R. Grumet in "The Plaintive Plaintiffs: Victims of the

Battered Child Syndrome," states:

The families of battered children are a study in deprivation, both physical and emotional. The families are usually
beset by problems such as marital problems, financial troubles,
alcoholism and mental illness. In many cases there are severe
neurotic or psychotic problems, or mental retardation on the
part of the abusing parents. . .In one study over one half the
abusing parents had been abused themselves. (Katz, 1974, p. 155)

She further describes these families as isolated with numerous social pro-

blems.

The number of neglected children subjected to court intervention is

diminishing, possibly due to the increased private agencies and the reluc-

tance of the judges to deny parental rights in all but the most serious cases.

Lisa Richette (1970) reports that in 1931, 71 per cent of the dependent and

neglected children were removed from their homes by court action; in 1967,

only 48 per cent were actually removed.

Comparison of Delinquents and Non-Delinquents

The recent furor over the association of neglected predelinquent

and children in our institutions and detention facilities has been discussed

by many. In Los Angeles County, as in many other jurisdictions, the separa-

tion of the three basic types of detained minors, when effected by all, has

been done according to the adjudicated definition, rather than according

to the behavior itself, or the treatment needs of the minor involved. Diane

Wakelin, employee of Hamburger Home for Girls, one of the institutions

for predelinquent or acting out minors, reported in an address to the Public

Social Services Commission, mentioned above, May 1974, that the actual

basic acting-out behavior of these predelinquent and neglicted minors is

the same. In Los Angeles, recent efforts have been made to house the minors detained under Section 601 separately from those under Section 602 (Section 600 minors have been housed separately for some time). This segregation is based only on the court section under which the minor is charged and is used only during periods of detention in the county facility.

Haskell and Yablonsky (1974) see that this does not result in differential treatment and that under Section 601 and 602, minors are treated as they are in other states--placed on probation, kept in detention, sent to county juvenile homes, ranches or camps, or sent to the California Youth Authority, the State's institution for juveniles.

According to the Crime Commission Report; as quoted by Gary Adams, for the:

> . . . large bulk of offenders, particularly the youthful, the first or minor offender, institutional commitments can cause more problems than they solve. Institutions tend to isolate offenders from society, both physically and psychologically, cutting them off from schools, jobs, families and other supportive influences and increasing the probability that the label of criminal will be indelibly impressed upon them. (Adams, undated, p. 14)

Lerman criticizes the mixing together of "delinquents without crimes and real delinquents" in detention centers and "reform schools" in that they provide the learning experiences and training ground for future detention. He describes these institutions as "the State's human garbage dump for taking care of all kinds of problem children, expecially the poor." (Danzin, 1973)

Haskell and Yablonsky (1974) found that once a minor is referred to court, he is regarded as delinquent by his family or other persons involved-

-police, court staff and anyone else knowing of the incident. Thus, before the actual court proceedings, he may be placed in a detention facility (the juvenile equivalent of incarceration). Here, he comes into contact with youths awaiting hearings on a wide variety of charges or who have been adjudicated as delinquent and are awaiting assignment to a correctional facility. The newly admitted minor is treated as a delinquent by the staff members and by his peers within the institution. John Milner, School of Social Work, University of Southern California, in an address to an Institute for Los Angeles County Children's Services (1975) reported that a large number of abused and neglected children who appear before the Juvenile Court feel they have come to the Court's attention because of their own actions. They feel that they must be bad, and their self-image becomes one of self hatred and often results in bizarre behavior in an attempt to get attention or affection.

According to Richette:

> . . . the more we brand children as delinquent, the less likely they are to respond positively to our ministrations. Many children become permanently antagonistic to authoritarian techniques; they form rigidly negative self images that lead to further anti-social behavior. (Richette, 1970, p. 315)

For this reason, the separation of delinquent and non-delinquent in the court system is recommended. Many studies have recommended that the status offenders not be subjected to the same court treatment as the law violators. Haskell and Yablonsky (1974) state that, especially in the case of runaways, cases should not result in arrests unless the child needs protection. They recommend citations for these petty law violators. As noted by Danzin (1973), these minors in detention with the more serious violators can learn that the occurrences that have been part of his life--squabbles at home, truancy, sexual promiscuity--are just as delinquent as stealing, robbery and assault. He sees that the elements of his life brought him to the same institution as the "delinquent" and, thus, his self image is created. Danzin goes on to state that if the status offenses are deleted from the juvenile court setting, certainly the neglected and dependent children should be removed from the system as well.

Summary

To summarize the prior research in the field of juvenile delinquency and youth neglect would be to write the history of known civilization. However, from the research, several theories consistently appear--sometimes in opposition to each other, but nevertheless offering some type of explanation. Ecological studies, showing higher degrees of delinquency in the inner cities were carried on by Shaw and McKay, Earl R. Moses (1941), Park Burgess et. al. (1925), and Sullenger (1936). These studies and theories found causation in the poverty, slum areas and lower class living of the inner city residents. Cloward and Chlin worked on what they called the "Opportunity Theory," finding delinquency and crime higher when individuals not having access to legitimate opportunities for gaining their goals, and having access to illegitimate methods of obtaining them, would resort to these illegitimate means.

The Gluecks' studies in the 1950's identified family elements as causative of delinquent tendencies. They related the use of physical punish-ment to later delinquent behavior and studied deviant aspects of delinquent's homes. Their conclusions tend to indicate influences in the family have a correlation with delinquency. Rejecting, disturbed, chaotic families tend to have delinquent boys.

Albert Cohen (1955), dealt with gangs and their origin from the asso-ciation and interaction of boys with similar problems in densely settled areas. He found status deprivation to be the greatest problem of the boy who becomes a member of a gang. Those individuals with no other access to status, choose the gang as a place to achieve importance.

Walter B. Miller (1958) placed value on the family and on social class. He asserted that lower class standards being different from those of the middle class, produced more delinquent behavior, but he further pointed out that the behavior is defined as delinquent by the middle class, not necessarily by the class from which the delinquent comes.

A British psychologist in 1952 attempted to relate juvenile delinquency to family trauma. He found mother separation among the group of thieves he studied. He found separation from parental affection produced "affec-tionate-less" delinquents. McCord and McCord (1959) found quarrelsome homes lead to more delinquency than broken homes.

Hirshi and Selvin (1966) stated while it may not be true that broken homes are a suffieient cause of delinquency, and that while there are other variables involved, broken homes surely still have a positive corre-lation to delinquency.

Browning (1966) found that one of the most important aspects of family relations, closely related to the concept of broken homes, is the quality of parental and marital adjustment and family solidarity. He found both of these bore a significant relationship to truancy and auto theft.

McKay and McKay found both parental rejection and the absence of maternal warmth were significantly related to delinquency.

Gerald J. Pine (1964) found a significant relationship between social class status and alcohol offenses, serious offenses and collective partici-pation in delinquent acts.

In summary, it seems that the causes of delinquency and the causes of court intervention for a minor's protection are the same. Roul Tunley (1962) notes that one reason delinquency appears higher in the slum areas is that the slum child is more visible and is much more quickly picked up for an offense than a middle class youngster would be for a similar offense. He quotes Stephen Holeman, of the Los Angeles County Probation Department, as reporting that:

> Kids who violated curfew in privileged Beverly Hills were taken to their homes by the police. Those who violated curfew in underprivileged East Los Angeles were taken to police headquarters. (Tunley, 1962, p. 91)

Gary B. Adams, et. al. (undated) shows the problems of youth, both for delinquents and for those who are brought to the attention of the court for neglect for minor violations. He views the need for dealing with juvenile behavior in four ways: (1) as a consequence of insufficient con-cern for youth and inadequate functioning of agencies to deal with them.

This is the role of the enabler; (2) as the failure of the social organizations. This is the idea of a power deficit--the delinquent feels powerless and needs a planner. This is the role of the advocate; (3) as a symptom of basic societal defects. The minor uses defensive or compensating strategies. Civil rights is the issue; (4) related to family or local community influences that create anti-social attitudes. These four areas describe the three types of minors to be dealt with under the current court system: the neglected child, the predelinquent and the delinquent.

William Kvaraceus (1954) stated, "Delinquent behavior is not the result of any innate perverseness. It is an attempt to meet some personal need or needs of the child." (Kvaraceus, 1954). Therefore, delinquency must be considered adjustive behavior from the point of view of the child. Delinquents as children of lower class families, have more frustration to deal with and get less help at home.

Thus, the elements of delinquency causation cover almost every element of life. Most studies point to several stronger causative elements: poverty; poor family relationships; poor home conditions; high incidence of criminality; mental retardation; emotional disturbances of the parents; more material privation; multiple and inconstant or inconsistent parental figures; female centered homes, giving no father figure for boys to utilize in their growth. Studies of the homes of abused and neglected children show similar problems. Howard James states, ". . . nearly every delinquent had an inadequate home." (James 1969, p. 21). Parents were too young, selfish or ignorant of their children's needs, were suffering from alcoholism, rejected their children. He further reported that these neglected, abused children are turned over to the Welfare Department, where delinquency is helped along. He states, "In many parts of the nation, children are locked behind bars by welfare workers -- not because the children have broken the law, but because they have been mistreated at home." (James, 1969, p. 23). He further describes the child whose father is a convict, or whose mother is on welfare, as having a lower self image, as has been said of delinquents.

All in all, the descriptions of behavior and background of delinquent, pre-delinquent and neglected children appear to be quite similar.

CHAPTER III

METHODOLOGY

This chapter describes the processes of administration of the KD Proneness test to minors in six settings: MacLaren Hall, Central Juvenile Hall, Los Padrinos Hall, Pacific Lodge, Maryvale and a metropolitan high school. This test was designed to determine proneness toward delinquency and was selected for its availability and simplicity of administration. The test itself was developed based on literature indicating a difference between delinquents and non-delinquents in: "family relationships, home conditions, location of residence, social and economic status, truancy record, school retardation, academic aptitude, school marks, liking for school, immaturity, club membership, companionship, family mobility, etc." (Scoring Key, Kvaraceus, 1950). Several neutral items are included, such as favorite drink, or color. The scale attempted to determine if delinquents respond differently than non-delinquents. In tests run in several eastern schools, test items found within the .05 criterion of significance were deemed acceptable. Items not acceptable were eliminated or unscored in the final test.

The Research Design

The testing process involved use of a multiple choice test administered is six locations to compare delinquency proneness of minors in varying stages of the Juvenile Court processes. A survey method was used, limited to minors present and willing in the six test sites. In order to run the test, permission of the Los Angeles County Probation and Public Social Services Departments was necessary, as well as that of the Presiding Judge of the Juvenile Court and the Los Angeles City Schools. Permission letters are appendixed.

The Sample

Test samples were minors detained under Sections 600, 601 and 602 of the California Welfare and Institutions Code, minors placed in treatment institutions, including both court supervised minors and minors placed there voluntarily by their parents, and a sample from a metropolitan high school with an ethnic balance similar to that of the institutionalized minors, though slightly skewed toward Mexican and Cuban extractions. The purpose of this study is to determine if differences exist between minors before, during and after the experience of court action and to determine if, in fact, the minors labeled "delinquent" by the court have more delinquent characteristics than non-delinquent minors in placement and in their own homes. Thus, the groups selected represent minors described under the three code sections as well as minors needing institutional treatment, but not under Court supervision.

The sample was limited to minors present and willing to take part on the days testing was done at the six locations. One minor having taken the test at MacLaren Hall and later being tested at Maryvale, was excluded from the second test.

The Procedure

As much as was possible, testing procedure was standardized in each of the six groups. Because the high school was used, an attempt was made to use a school or school-like setting for the other groups; however, only at MacLaren Hall and Maryvale was the actual school used. The other settings were limited by school hours and permission of the Board of Education.

The first group tested was at MacLaren Hall. The test was given in the school, in three separate groups, boys and girls together, and was prefaced by a statement explaining there were no right or wrong answers and one could not fail; further, we were trying to better understand young people and this test was one way of gaining that understanding. This preface was the same at all six locations. Minors were given pencils and asked to circle their answers. As the literacy rate was somewhat low, and due to some of the outdated terminolody, the test administrator was available to answer questions and/or explain meanings of words. The mood of the classroom was relaxed and minors were not subjected to any disciplinary rules. When finished, minors stayed in the classroom and class resumed when all were finished.

The second group tested was the high school. Testing was done in the cafeteria at Physical Education times, two large classes, boy and girls together. Here again, the opening statement was given and minors were free to ask questions of the examiner at any time. When finished, minors waited until the entire class was finished and then went with teachers to the class.

At Central Juvenile Hall, minors were brought into the room by staff members, 601's, boys and girls, in one group, and 602 boys in another. Here the groups were tested in a conference room, having been escorted in by a staff member responsible for them. This group was considered less representative than the others, only three of the 601's being boys, and the overall number being small; however, testing was limited to those minors available on the test date. After the test, minors waited while their counselor was called to escort them to their respective classes.

Testing at Pacific Lodge Boys' Home was one in three groups at two separate times. This was done in order to get boys in three different cottages. Testing here was done in late afternoon since all the boys there attend public school. The atmosphere here was different from the other test facilities due to the time and setting, which was more home-like. Initial instructions were given in a lounge, and minors retired to their rooms to complete the test. The administrator circulated among them to answer questions. Upon completion, minors were free to resume evening activities.

Testing at Maryvale was again in an on-grounds school setting, with all the girls together in a lounge for initial explanation and free to ask questions as needed. Girls went to classrooms to complete the test and the test administrator circulated among them. Upon completion, minors remained in the classrooms.

At Los Padrinos Hall, testing was done at night in a large room with tables. These minors were Section 602 girls only. They were free to ask questions as needed. Upon completion, they returned to their rooms.

The KD Proneness test was the only data gathering method used. Data were not available from any other source due to confidentiality of records of the Juvenile Court and the institutions and agencies involved in their supervision. The choice of institutions was determined merely by the author's personal experience with the institutions and their interest and willingness to participate. Several other institutions were contacted initially; however, their reaction was guarded and it was decided to limit the study to those chosen. The purpose of the study was discussed with staff members at all facilities, and all expressed interest in the comparison of delinquent and non-delinquent minors as defined by the court. The consensus of those contacted was that minors coming to the attention of the Juvenile Court, either due to neglect, status offenses or penal code offenses, as well as those placed in institutions by their parents without court intervention (in most cases due to parent-child conflicts involving incorrigibility), have a similar delinquency proneness. A common statement was, "it just depends on who catches them first.

The Variables

The test instrument itself measures delinquency on a scale of plus and minus zero. Plus scores indicate delinquent tendencies, minus scores indicate non-delinquent tendencies. There are 75 questions on the test, each with four possible answers, 83 answers considered plus and 55 considered minus for boys, and 58 plus and 43 minus for girls. The remaining items were found inconclusive and were omitted from the scoring. It should be noted that many of the questions have more than one answer receiving a plus or minus score. For instance, on question number 4 for boys, answers 2 and 3 generate a plus count, while answer 4 results in a minus count. Copies of scoring keys are appendixed. There were several differences in scoring between boys and girls, including such items as success in school, reactions to violence in others and future educational plans. These items are given merit in the boy's scoring, but they are omitted from the girl's.

The Statistical Procedure

Data were hand scored using the pre-coded answer sheets with different codes for boys and girls. The data is organized into charts indicating scores on a scale of plus to minus. Frequency of scores on this scale is indicated as is mean score per location and standard deviation. The F test for significance was applied using data processing equipment.

Additional Data Processing Procedure

An item analysis was obtained through the use of data processing and correlation of answer choice given for various locations. Partial data processing information is included in the appendix; the entire analysis is too great to include for this research, although it was used to notify the institutions involved of their particular interests and answers.

The Pilot Study

Due to the confidential nature of records and the limited number of minors available, a pilot study was not deemed feasible.

Summary

In summary, the methodology in this study involved administration of a pre-developed test, which had been evaluated for reliability factors, to determine delinquency proneness in minors under supervision of the Juvenile Court under Sections 600, 601 and 602 of the Welfare and Institutions Code and supervised by the Los Angeles County Probation and Public Social Services Departments. This single test instrument, the KD Proneness test, has been developed as a result of studies in the late forties.

An effort was made to standardize testing procedure to insure accuracy and consistency.

The language of the test itself was found to be a problem in some instances, due to out-of-date slang usage and the low literacy rate of many of the minors involved. Such words as "crooner," and "mischief," and "success" and failure" were difficult for some minors to understand. The test administrator was careful to explain these terms and answer any questions. Two questions involved statements about "girlfriends" and "boyfriends." There was confusion on the part of the minors as to the connotations of these terms; however, the two questions involved have been omitted from the score keys.

41

An interesting note involves the minors' feelings about taking the test. They were enthusiastic and eager to take part. There was much concern on the part of the court and the agencies involved to maintain confidentiality; however, most minors, particularly those under court supervision, asked to be allowed to write their names on the tests. Although this was discouraged, many wrote their names in anyway. This may indicate their concern with establishing identity, identity deemed "confidential" by the agencies involved.

CHAPTER IV

PRESENTATION OF THE DATA

The purpose of this chapter is to present comparative data of this study as obtained from the test administration. The major focus will be comparison of scores, on a scale of plus to minus 20. The respondents were the minors tested in the six locations: MacLaren Hall, Central Juvenile Hall, Los Padrinos Hall, Maryvale, Pacific Lodge, and the high school, regarding delinquency proneness and the differences between sex, location and code section involved. Further a partial item analysis is included, giving comparative data pertaining to pertinent questions. The purpose of the test was to test the null hypothesis, as described in Chapter I, that there is no significant difference in delinquency proneness among minors under supervision of the Juvenile Court under Sections 600, 601 and 602 of the Welfare and Institutions Code.

Descriptive Data

This section contains a descriptive analysis of delinquency proneness scores on minors tested. Table I gives raw score comparison for all minors tested. It may be noted that the total population tested (259) shows a mean score of -2.67. High positive score would show minors who have high delinquency proneness. The negative overall score would indicate low delinquency proneness.

Tables II through VI give a comparison of the scores of the different groups.

TABLE I

Score	Total	600 Boys	600 Girls	600 Total	601 Boys	601 Girls	601 Total	602 Boys	602 Girls	602 Total	Maryvale	Pacific Lodge	High School Boys	High School Girls	High School Total
+16-17	1														
+14-15	1	1													
+12-13	1														
+10-11	1			1					1	1					
+8-9	3							1		3	1				
+6-7	15	1	1	2		3	3	5	2	9	3	1			
+4-5	12	4	1	2	1	2	3	1	4	1	4	2	2	2	4
+2-3	16		3	4	1	1	2	2	1	3	3	2	2	6	8
0-1	25		3	1	1	2	3	3	3	6	1	6	3	3	6
-1-2	23	1	6	3		1	1	2	3	5	10	4	4	7	11
-3-4	39	2		4		2	2	3	1	4	5	4	8	6	14
-5-6	29		1	8				2	4	6	8	5	4	8	12
-7-8	30			1				1	3	4	1	7	3	4	7
-9-10	20	2		2				1	2	3	2	2	6	2	8
-11-12	14	1	1	2							1	2	3	3	7
-13-14	11		1	1								3	3	1	4
-15-16	10		1	1							2				1
-17-18	4		1	1					1	1		1	2	1	2
-19-20	4	1		1								1		1	
-21-22	1											1			
N		13	19	32	3	11	14	21	26	47	41	41	40	44	84
True* Mean		-1.77	-4.26		+2.67	+1.91		+0.48	-0.65	-0.15	-4.17	-7.10	-7.10	-5.98	-6.82
S.D.		10.01	7.55	9.95	3.01	6.60	6.44	8.61	10.80	9.90	13.03	15.93	16.96	14.46	15.71

* True Mean shown varies somewhat from mean scores used in F Test which utilizes midpoint mean.

TOTAL RAW SCORES FOR ALL GROUPS TESTED ON KD PRONENESS SCALE

45

TABLE II*
SECTION 600 MINORS
MacLaren Hall

Score	Boys	Girls	Total
+16-17			
+14-15			
+12-13	1		1
+10-11			
+8-9			
+6-7	1	1	2
+4-5	4		4
+2-3		1	1
0-1		3	3
-1-2	1	3	4
-3-4	2	6	8
-5-6			
-7-8		1	1
-9-10	2		2
-11-12	1	1	2
-13-14		1	1
-15-16		1	1
-17-18		1	1
-19-20	1		1
N	13	19	32
Mean	-1.77	-4.26	-3.38
S.D.	10.01	7.55	9.95

*See page 51 for analysis of Tables II through VI

TABLE III
SECTION 601 MINORS
Central Juvenile Hall

Score	Boys	Girls	Total
+16-17			
+14-15			
+12-13			
+10-11			
+8-9			
+6-7		3	3
+4-5	1	2	3
+2-3	1	1	2
0-1	1	2	3
-1-2		1	1
-3-4		2	2
-5-6			
-7-8			
-9-10			
-11-12			
-13-14			
-15-16			
-17-18			
-19-20			
N	3	11	14
Mean	+2.67	+1.91	+2.07
S.D.	3.01	6.60	6.44

COMPARATIVE SCORES
KD PRONENESS SCALE

TABLE IV
SECTION 602 MINORS
Central Juvenile Hall and Los Padrinos Hall

	Total	Boys	Girls
+16-17	1		
+14-15			
+12-13			
+10-11	1		
+8-9	3	1	2
+6-7	9	5	4
+4-5	1	1	
+2-3	3	2	1
0-1	6	3	3
-1-2	5	2	3
-3-4	4	3	1
-5-6	6	2	4
-7-8	4	1	3
-9-10	3	1	2
-11-12			
-13-14			
-15-16			
-17-18	1		1
-19-20			
-21-22			
N	47	21	26
Mean	-0.15	+10.48	-0.65
S.D.	9.90	8.61	10.80

TABLE V
MINORS IN PLACEMENT

	Maryvale Girls	Pacific Lodge Boys
+16-17		
+14-15		
+12-13		
+10-11		
+8-9		
+6-7	1	
+4-5	3	1
+2-3	4	2
0-1	3	2
-1-2	1	6
-3-4	10	4
-5-6	5	4
-7-8	8	5
-9-10	1	7
-11-12	2	2
-13-14	1	2
-15-16	2	3
-17-18		1
-19-20		1
-21-22		1
N	41	41
Mean	-4.17	-7.10
S.D.	13.03	15.93

COMPARATIVE SCORES
KD PRONENESS SCALE

TABLE VI

HIGH SCHOOL STUDENTS

	Boys	Girls	Total
+16-17			
+14-15			
+12-13			
+10-11			
+8-9			
+6-7			
+4-5			
+2-3	2	2	4
0-1	2	6	8
-1-2	3	3	6
-3-4	4	7	11
-5-6	8	6	14
-7-8	4	8	12
-9-10	3	4	7
-11-12	6	2	8
-13-14	3	4	7
-15-16	3	1	4
-17-18		1	1
-19-20			
-21-22	2		2
N	40	44	84
Mean	-7.85	-5.98	-6.92
S.D.	16.96	14.46	15.71

Table II, relating to minors detained under Section 600 of the Welfare and Institutions Code, for their protection, shows a mean raw score of -3.38 for the 32 minors tested, girls scoring more negatively than boys.

Table III, the 601 minors, normally not considered seriously delinquent, but exhibiting some anti-social characteristics, shows a mean score of +2.07, the only group showing a positive score. However, the small size of the population may skew the figures somewhat.

Table IV, the 602's, shows scores slightly less than the 601's and with a total mean score of -.15.

Table V compares minors at the two institutions, Maryvale for girls and Pacific Lodge for boys. Here both groups show relatively low proneness, only slightly less than the lowest group, the high school students, shows in Table VI.

Correlation Analysis

An item analysis was done for all 75 test items by use of Data Processing techniques. Age differences are shown in Table VII.

TABLE VII

Age breakdown of all groups tested:

Group	10	11	12	13	14	Age 15	16	17	18	19	20	Not given
600-boys			1		4	2	4	2				
600-girls			1	3	3	3	5	2				2
601-boys						1	2					
601-girls					2	6	1	2				
602-boys	1			1	5	7	6	1				
602-girls			2	1	1	7	9	5				1
Maryvale			2	4	10	10	10	5				
Pacific Lodge			1	4	7	12	14	2				1
High School-boys						3	9	18	7	1		2
High School-girls					1	4	15	16	3			4

Several test questions were particularly interesting. Questions 3 and 4 relating to success in school, showed a general agreement on the part of most that school is necessary. On question 8, whether or not parents understand their children, minors seem to vary between "well" and "not very well," 2 and 3 on a scale of 1 to 4. On question 23, whether or not school work is difficult, the non-delinquent high school students seemed more comfortable with school. Their literacy rate is presumed to be higher. There seemed to be more minors in the court group who find school work difficult. While many in this group also describe work as very easy, the group also has higher numbers of minors out of school or in special classes.

Cheating is not uncommon according to question 29. 32.6 per cent claim most students cheat, and 12 per cent claim all students cheat. Attitudes towards police were quite good according to questions 27 and 63, although the minors with higher proneness and those with prior court involvement were more skeptical.

On question 52, most minors felt that they had been lucky to some degree. Here, the boys seemed to feel better than the girls, the detained delinquents and pre-delinquents less lucky than the others. Item analysis of selected questions if included in the Appendix.

Inferential Statistics

The F test for analysis of variance was applied to the data from the varying samples to determine if the difference between them was significant at the .01 level. Table VIII illustrates the results for the four large groups: 600's, 601's, 602's and the control group of high school students. These were analyzed first to determine whether the null hypothesis that there are no significant differences between these groups should be retained.

TABLE VIII

Source	SS	DF	MS +	F
Total	8173.73	175		
Between Groups	1930.05	3	643.35	17.72**
Within Groups	6243.68	172	36.30	

** f .01 level
$F_{.05}$ = 2.66, f .05
$F_{.01}$ = 3.8955, f .01

+ means determined through midpoint scores as detailed in Table I vary somewhat from the true mean shown in that table.

Based on this, the null hypothesis can be rejected at the .01 level. The f score of 17.72 exceeds the $F_{.01}$ of 3.8955.

Further comparison was made, including all ten groups: 600 boys, 600 girls, 601 boys, 601 girls, 602 boys, 602 girls, Maryvale, Pacific Lodge, high school boys, high school girls. Table IX gives overall results:

TABLE IX

Summary Table

Source	SS	DF	MS	F
Total	11128.831	258.0		
Between Groups	2232.183	9.0	248.02033	6.9416101**
Within Groups	8896.648	249.0	35.72951	

$F_{.05}$ = 1.915, f .05

**$F_{.01}$ = 2.49, f .01

Again, the null hypothesis can be rejected at the .01 level. Significant

differences do exist among the groups and can be considered not to have

occurred through chance. The research hypothesis is accepted, neces-

sitating further study and analysis of the specific differences and treat-

ment needs.

Summary

This study was done to test the null hypothesis that there are no

significant differences in delinquency proneness among minors detained

and supervised under Sections 600, 601 and 602 of the Welfare and

Institutions Code. The KD Proneness Scale was administered to these

groups and handscored, using precoded keys to determine a plus or

minus score. The resulting scores were compared for the groups tested.

Low negative scores indicate low delinquency proneness, high positive

scores indicate higher delinquency proneness. Based on data available,

the F test was applied to determine validity.

In summary, raw scores were compared among the different types of minors. These indicate delinquent proneness is highest in Section 601 minors, with 602 second and then 600. Those in placement scored lower and the high school students lowest. The F test was applied and the null hypothesis was rejected at the .01 level, indicating there are significant differences between these groups. The research hypothesis is accepted as tenable and leads to recommendations for further study.

CHAPTER V

INTERPRETATIONS, CONCLUSIONS AND RECOMMENDATIONS

The purpose of this chapter is to interpret and evaluate the findings of the study relating to the hypothesis described in Chapter I. In addition, some recommendations are made for further study, and an evaluation of the test vehicle is included.

Interpretation of the Data

To determine if indeed differences do exist between delinquent, pre-delinquent and non-delinquent minors in detention and in placement under the supervision of the Los Angeles County Juvenile Court, the test results for the KD Proneness Scale were compared and evaluated using the F test for analysis of variance. Scores were found to be significantly different between the groups at the .01 level. This results in rejection of the null hypothesis and the necessity for further study to evaluate the needs of these minors. From the analysis of variance, we can assume that there are differences in delinquency proneness between the various types of minors under Court supervision. Further study should reveal the extent of those differences and possibly provide insight into the methods best suited to dealing with them.

Some limits may have bearing on the score validity. The varying sizes of the groups may have some effect on both the raw score of the individual minor and the group itself. Since only three 601 boys and eleven 601 girls were tested, this group is considered too small to utilize as accurately as the other groups. Differences were seen in the attitudes of the minors in the larger settings. The larger groups tended to be more unstructured, and the general attitude of the minors was less formal. However, these larger groups also tended to ask more questions and display more interest. An additional validity problem is the lack of understanding of terms by the minors. However, the groups all had trouble with similar words, resulting at least, in consistent answers.

The test data seems to indicate differences in delinquency proneness as would be expected by the status of the minors. Those minors detained for status crimes tended to score slightly higher in proneness than the minors accused of more serious law violations; however, the difference may not be greatly significant, particularly since the number of status crime offenders tested was small. This would support the theory that the "601" minors, most of whom are detained for runaway or incorrigibility, have similar attitudes to the minors having been detained for the more serious offenses. Both groups having gone through the process of detention, having been arrested and been administered their rights, having been before the court and ordered "locked up," tend to answer questions meeting the definition being given them--that of delinquent. The attitude of the 601's becomes complicated by the fact that they are punished just as much as those who have committed more serious crimes. Their attitude tends to reflect their feelings that they are not getting a fair shake.

The minors at MacLaren Hall, also having been detained and before the Court, tend to show more delinquency proneness than the general population, but do, in fact, score negatively on the scale. However, their scores are not as low as the test group. These minors having been subjected to traumatizing situations, are perhaps beginning to show signs of delinquenct proneness. It should be noted that many of the minors at MacLaren Hall are there because they have run away from placement facilities after Court intervention under Section 600. When they return to MacLaren Hall, they may have been in placement for long periods of time or may have failed in numerous prior placements. Here, as with the status offenders, the behavior is being described as predelinquent by those working with the minor, even though Section 601 is not invoked. This definition is known to the minor and may lead to his self-definition as delinquent. Many of these minors, already under Section 600 supervision, avoid further Court filing since the Court tends to feel they will function as well with 600 supervision as with 601 or 602.

The scores of the minors at the placement facilities tend to be slightly higher than the control group of high school students, but the differences are quite slight. It would appear that the experience of the treatment facility has resulted in the decreasing of delinquent tendencies, not only in the 601 and 602 minors, but also in the 600 minors. This supports the theory that the treatment facility should be designed to deal with the individual minor's needs rather than with the Court's definition of behavior. The experience of intermixing has resulted in lessened scores for all three groups, indicating that the counseling received rather than peer group pressure has been effective.

Finally, the data indicate some differences between adjudicated delinquents and neglected minors. However, it also indicates no detriment in mixing these minors in a therapeutic setting.

Conclusions

This study tends to indicate some differences in minors under Court supervision in Los Angeles County. The initial thought had been that few differences exist and that those differences that are present are not relevant to a decision as to the treatment modality needed for the minor involved. The data appears to indicate some differences, particularly in minors tested during the detention period. Here the 601's followed, and the 600's after them. The raw scores for the minors in placement were only slightly less negative than the high school control group, indicating a lessening of delinquent proneness after placement. Some limitations of the test should be mentioned. Probably the biggest obstacle was the language. The age of the test resulted in some archaic word use, and minors were not able to understand some questions. As indicated in the review of literature, many of the minors coming to the attention of the Juvenile Court, having been through difficult times or coming from families in trouble, have received less education and, therefore, are less literate than those who have not suffered these problems. It was for this reason that an attempt was made to locate a control group high school with a lower than average socio-economic population and with an ethnic mix as found in Court minors. Despite this, the high school students tended to understand the test better. However, the minors in the placement facilities, who it should be noted were at the time of the test in school and receiving counseling also appeared to understand. Possibly as a result, these two groups were able to "psych" the test and their scores were lower.

An additional element in question is the effect of the detention process itself. During this time minors in all three facilities are, in essence, locked up, have their personal effects taken from them and do not have freedom to do as they wish or have any real social activities. This would seem to have an effect on their morale and, consequently on their test scores. For this reason it is felt by this writer that the actual delinquent proneness, particularly for the Section 600 and 601 minors, would be somewhat lower in a different setting.

It is this writer's opinion, based upon professional experience with the minors involved, that while certain differences may exist between the three categories of Court supervised minors, these cannot be assumed to (a) result in any set behavior patterns; (b) be indicative of the type of care and treatment needed; or (c) be as concise as the code sections. This study would support the need for keeping the Section 600 minors separate during the detention period as their attitudes at that time seem to be somewhat better than the 601 and 602 minors. However, the treatment and/or rehabilitation needs of all three groups seem to depend on the individual minor and, for this reason, separation in non-secure placement facilities should be on the basis of need. The fact that when this is done as it is at the two

59

facilities tested, the delinquency proneness is less, indicates this.

Recommendations for Further Study

Since there is great emphasis at present in keeping detained minors in separate facilities according to their Court status, while placement agencies recognize a different method of housing minors, further study should be made in the area of behavior analysis and treatment modality needed. The cost of maintaining separate detention facilities is high and it would seem that if indeed the intermixture is detrimental to the minors, the separation should be maintained in placement facilities as well as detention centers, making the cost even higher. However, there is an indication from data collected that those minors in the two placement facilities tended to have a reduced delinquency potential, possibly resulting from the treatment program in effect. This would indicate that the treatment modality rather than the Court status or peer group influence is having a positive effect. A further complicating element involves the population of the two institutions: Court and non-Court. Due to the restrictions placed on this research by the probation and Public Social Service Departments and the Juvenile Court, it was not possible to determine if the scores on 600, 601 and 602 minors as well as non-Court supervised minors, differed before and after placement.

Based on these elements, further study is indicated with an emphasis on "before and after" scores and involving release of more information about the minors involved. An updated version of the test should be used, with appropriate language changes. This was found to be a problem and several test questions have become invalide due to archaic language or changed meanings of words.

A longitudinal study could be of great benefit in determining effectiveness of the detention and placement processes in helping minors work through adjustment problems and prepare for adult life. Certainly this study indicates some need to provide a method of evaluating minors prior to Court intervention. The lack of significant differences in many areas would tend to indicate a need to redefine "delinquency" in the Court system. Many minors are labeled "delinquent" by the Court for actions common to most adolescents, but for which most never come to the attention of any police agency as families are available to intercede. Conversely, many of the Section 600 minors have actually violated other code sections but have been continued under Section 600 rather than being readjudicated under Sections 601 or 602. It is in these cases that the Court definition becomes hazy. It seems that the minors currently under the supervision of the Juvenile Court constitute only a small proportion of the minors who have engaged in "delinquent" acts. Further study of this segment of the population may show a better system for treatment of juvenile offenders. Certainly an evaluation of the effect of detention itself needs to be made. The fact that neglected minors score higher while in detention than the placed minors, may indicate some detrimental aspects of the process in the development of the minors' self concepts. For this reason it is recommended that further in-depth study be done on the entire detention and placement process for delinquent and non-delinquent minors.

Appendix I

Juvenile-Mental Health Departments
THE SUPERIOR COURT
210 West Temple Street
Los Angeles, California   90012

October 10, 1975

Mrs. Phyllis Levine
11850 Old River School Road
Downey, California   90241

Dear Ms. Levine:

I have received your letter of September 17th requesting permission to administer a delinquency proneness test to certain minors. This letter is to authorize your contact with wards and dependents of the court in furtherance of legitimate research. This authorization is contingent upon your making satisfactory arrangements directly with the Probation Department as to the implementation of your project so that it does not interfere with the necessary work being performed by that organization on county time. Minors' names and other menas of identification shall not be disclosed.

Very truly yours,

COUNTY OF LOS ANGELES
Probation Department
Box 4002 Terminal Annex
Los Angeles, California   90052

October 28, 1975

Ms. Phyllis Levine
11850 Old River School Road
Downey, California   90241

Dear Ms. Levine:

I am pleased to inform you that your plan for a study of delinquency has been approved by Mr. Gordon Pedersen, Assistant Probation Officer.

I would be happy to work with you in arranging the details of the study at Central Juvenile Hall. Please contact me at 923-7721, extension 2534, at your convenience.

Very truly yours,

DEPARTMENT OF PUBLIC SOCIAL SERVICES
Bureau of Special Operations

June 17, 1975

TO: Bureau of Social Services

FROM: Research and Statistical Section

SUBJECT: Research Request for Study of Children at MacLaren Hall

This is in response to your memo of June 12. I agree with you that the proposed study by Phyllis Levine of children at MacLaren Hall has merit. Attached you will find two forms related to the approval of outside research requests.

>   -The first describes the overall requirements, one
>   important element of which is the researcher's
>   agreement to provide the Department "with a
>   complete report of the results of the research."

>   -The second is a "Declaration of Confidentiality."
>   Please have the researcher complete this form and
>   have it notarized.

The plan has our approval upon our receipt of the notarized "Declaration of Confidentiality."

Also, if Ms. Levine's report is not too bulky, I would appreciate a copy. However, if you only receive one copy, I would appreciate having an opportunity to review it. Let me know if I can be of any further assistance.

LOS ANGELES CITY UNIFIED SCHOOL DISTRICT
Administrative Offices: 450 North Grand Avenue, Los Angeles, California

August 29, 1975

Ms. Phyllis Levine
11850 Old River School Road #4
Downey, California 90241

Dear Ms. Levine:

The Committee on Research Studies has approved your request to conduct a study with the descriptive title "Predelinquent Tendencies in 14-18 Year Olds" in the Los Angeles Unified School District. Your study is restricted to   High School.

This approval by the Committee on Research Studies is in no way a requirement for District personnel to participate. The approval of your study is contingent upon the use of a single measure, the KD Proneness Scale. All participation by the principal, staff, and pupils must be completely voluntary. The anonymity of all participants and the school must be maintained.

You may use this letter as an authorization to approach the principal who may wish to participate in your study. At the conclusion of the study, please send an abstract of the findings to the Committee.

                              Sincerely,

Appendix II

A.S.M. - VOL. II

CASE

PROCEDURES

<u>REASON FOR REFERRAL (ALLEGATIONS) CODES</u>

602's

02 - Arson (447 PC)
03 - Assault (217, 220, 221, 240 PC)
04 - Assault/Weapon (244, 245 PC)
05 - Battery (242, 243 PC)
07 - Burglary (459, 464 PC)
10 - Checks/NSF-Forgery (470-475a, 476a&b, 477-480, 484a PC, 4463 VC)
14 - Curfew (-----)
15 - Dangerous Weapons (417, 12020, 12021, 12025, 4502 PC)
16 - Dist. Peace/Disord. Conduct (415, 647c, e, h, PC)
17 - Drunk (647f PC)
20 - Drunk Driving (23101 & 23102 VC)
22 - Fraud (532a, b; 72 PC)
23 - Fail to Obey Court Order (-----)
24 - Glue Sniffing (647f)
25 - Hit/Run Vehicle (20001 & 20002 VC)
26 - Homosexual Acts (288A, 286 PC)
27 - Indecent Exposure (314 PC)
30 - L & L Acts on Child (Child Molesting) (288 PC)
32 - Liquor Violations (25658, 25668 E & P)
33 - Mal. Mischief/Trespessing (594, 602 PC)
34 - Manslaughter (192, 192.1, 192.3a/b PC)
36 - Murder (187, 189 PC)
38 - Obscene Matter (pornography) (311 PC)
40 - Possession of Dangerous Drugs (11540, 11910 H & S)
41 - Possession of Dangerous Drugs for Sale (11911 H & S)
42 - Selling, Transporting, Furnishing Dangerous Drugs (11912, 11913 H & S)
43 - Possession of Marijuana (11530 H & S)
44 - Possession Marijuana for Sale (11530.5 H & S)
45 - Selling, Transporting, Furnishing Marijuana (11531, 11532 H & S)
46 - Possession, Use of Narcotics (11500, 11721, H & S)

REASON FOR REFERRAL (ALLEGATIONS) CODES - continued

47 - Possession Narcotics for Sale (11500, 11721 H & S)
48 - Sale, Transport, Furnishing Narcotics (11501, 11503 H & S)
49 - Misc. Drug, Including Forging Prescription Paraphernalia
      (11170.5, 11850-11851 H & S: 4230, 4390, 9237 H & P:
      Other H & S and B & P Codes)
50 - Prostitution or Visiting (647b PC)
53 - Receiving Stolen Property (496a PC)
54 - Resisting an Officer (148 PC)
55 - Riot (404 and 405 PC)
56 - Robbery (211, 211a PC)
57 - Other Sex Offenses (------)
60 - Tampering with Auto (10852 VC)
61 - Theft Auto & Joyriding (487.3, 499b PC and 10851 VC)
62 - Theft, Grand (487.1 PC)
63 - Theft, Petty (484, 488 PC)
64 - Traffic Violations - Moving (-----)
65 - Traffic Violations - Non-Moving (-----)
66 - Unemployment Insurance Act (-----)
90 - Miscellaneous Felonies (Various Codes)
96 - Miscellaneous Misdemeanors (Various Codes)

601's   Tendencies

70 - Beyond Control of Parents - Incorrigible
71 - Beyond Control of School Officials
72 - In Danger of Leading Lewd, Immoral Life
73 - Runaway
74 - Transient
75 - Truancy
76 - All Other Delinquent Tendencies (601 W.I.C.)

600's   Dependents

80 - No Parent or Guardian
81 - No Parent or Guardian Willing to Exercise Control
82 - No Parent or Guardian Actually Exercising Control
83 - Unfit Home - Neglect
84 - Unfit Home - Cruelty
85 - Unfit Home - Depravity
86 - Unfit Home - Requires Medical Consent or Treatment
87 - Physically Dangerous
88 - All Other Dependent Child Situations (600 A,B,C,W.I.C.)

REASON FOR REFERRAL (ALLEGATIONS) CODES - continued

Civil Matters

91 - Abandonment
92 - Guardianship
93 - Custody
94 - All Others

REASON FOR REFERRAL BY TYPE CASE

REFERRAL REASON	CNT TOTAL	CNT NEW	CNT SUBSEQUENT
	3	2	1
01	2	1	1
02	33	24	9
03	156	115	41
04	690	564	126
05	693	575	118
07	2301	1801	500
09	1	1	0
10	39	31	8
14	165	136	29
15	322	253	69
16	168	123	45
17	236	174	62
20	316	261	55
22	2	2	0
24	137	111	26
25	27	22	5
26	16	16	0
27	12	9	3
30	48	44	4
32	83	65	18
33	312	269	43
34	12	11	1
36	70	40	30
38	1	1	0
40	83	73	10
41	9	9	0
42	5	5	0
43	835	721	114
44	99	93	6
45	7	6	1
46	58	45	13
47	13	11	2
48	7	5	2
49	151	135	16
50	26	21	5
51	59	43	16
52	6	5	1
53	197	153	44
54	147	117	30

REASON FOR REFERRAL BY TYPE CASE

Continued

REFERRAL REASON	CNT TOTAL	CNT NEW	CNT SUBSEQUENT
55	11	10	1
56	506	617	189
57	1	1	0
60	47	36	11
61	825	581	244
62	281	220	61
63	707	566	141
64	99	81	18
65	2	1	1
70	564	484	80
71	10	10	0
73	404	326	78
74	2	2	0
75	195	171	24
76	24	13	11
84	1	1	0
85	1	0	1
90	4	4	0
94	2	2	0
96	451	302	149
99	1	1	0
FINAL TOTALS	11985	9522	2463

11985 ENTRIES QUALIFY

REASON FOR REFERRAL BY TYPE CASE

REFERRAL REASON	CNT TOTAL	CNT NEW	CNT SUBSEQUENT
	10	8	2
88	3	3	0
0	1	0	1
00	2	2	0
02	39	36	3
03	129	96	33
04	714	574	138
05	611	497	114
07	2424	1915	509
08	1	1	0
10	33	30	3
14	178	142	36
15	309	244	65
16	247	193	54
17	232	169	63
20	347	299	48
22	2	2	0
24	138	109	29
25	52	43	9
26	17	13	4
27	14	12	2
30	44	38	6
32	124	99	25
33	326	267	59
34	15	13	2
36	78	56	22
40	49	36	13
41	10	10	0
42	8	6	2
43	869	730	139
44	157	142	15
45	24	22	2
46	52	40	12
47	21	21	0
48	13	13	0
49	148	132	16
50	26	24	2
51	29	18	11
52	2	1	1
53	204	161	43

REASON FOR REFERRAL BY TYPE CASE

Continued

REFERRAL REASON	CNT TOTAL	CNT NEW	CNT SUBSEQUENT
54	112	89	23
55	2	2	0
57	23	18	5
59	1	1	0
60	61	52	9
61	838	598	240
62	356	288	68
63	766	610	156
64	122	102	20
65	6	5	1
70	601	540	61
71	1	0	1
73	348	299	49
74	9	8	1
75	110	82	28
76	28	11	17
83	1	0	1
90	1	0	1
96	676	478	198
99	1	0	1
FINAL TOTALS	12549	10002	2547

12549 ENTRIES QUALIFY

Appendix III

REGION V

PACIFIC LODGE BOYS' HOME   RATE: Contract
4900 Serrania Avenue
WOODLAND HILLS, CALIFORNIA 91364   LICENSED BY: SDSW

Graduate Cottage
22362 Burbank Boulevard
WOODLAND HILLS, CALIFORNIA
CAPACITY: 6 Boys

Dolorosa Cottage
22357 Dolorosa Avenue
WOODLAND HILLS, CALIFORNIA
CAPACITY: 6 Boys

COUNTY: Los Angeles

AUSPICES: Private - Non-Profit

DIRECTOR: Wallace B. Wilson

CAPACITY: 83 Boys Aged 13-15 at Intake

LENGTH OF STAY: 18 Months

INTAKE: Consider each boy and his total problems and func-
                    tioning. Cannot accept boy with confirmed pattern
                    of homosexuality. Minimum placement of eight
                    months a condition of placement. Contact Central
                    Intake Worker. Submit written summary, includ-
                    ing medical and social information, school records;
                    psychological testing and psychiatric evaluation, if
                    done. Preplacement visit includes child and place-
                    ment worker.

EDUCATION: On-grounds EH class with accredited teacher, paid
                    aides, and volunteer aides. Tutoring available as
                    needed. Variety of school programs, including
                    vocational guidance and skills, available through
                    community school programs.

TREATMENT:

Well-integrated group living program in three large on-grounds cottages and two group homes in the near-by community. Also six beds in special cottage for emergency short-term placement and a "Graduate" apartment on grounds. MSW supervises total treatment program, gives consultation to the experienced, concerned child-care staff, holds mandatory group therapy in each cottage, does individual counselling with each boy, and with families if involved, including home visit if indicated. Weekly meeting with total cottage staff, SW and psychiatrist review each boy's functioning and treatment program monthly. Psychiatrist does consultation with total staff, sees boy directly for medication and/or crises. Two community group homes staffed by home parents and assigned social worker focus on emancipation skills, including work and/or vocational training, daily living activities, and socialization. Consistent program also for meeting medical and dental needs of all the boys.

RECREATION:

On-grounds indoor and outdoor games and play equipment, including gym and swimming pool. Trips to beach, camping, athletic events. Encourage boys to participate in community recreational and social activities.

5/7/74

MARYVALE
7600 East Graves Avenue
ROSEMEAD, CALIFORNIA 91770
(213) 380-6510

RATE: Contract

LICENSED BY: SDSW

COUNTY: Los Angeles

AUSPICES:	Private - Daughters of Charity, a non-profit Organization
DIRECTOR:	Sister Mary Elizabeth, D.C.
CAPACITY:	Total: 85 Children 73 Girls, 3 through 18 Years 12 Boys, 3 through 11 Years
LENGTH OF STAY:	12 Months Average
INTAKE:	Most all children/adolescents with behavior problems will be given serious consideration for placement. Telephone screening by Social Service Department secretary. Director of Social Services or a staff social worker, will return the call. Complete referral packet may be requested. An intake conference will be scheduled if placement if feasible.
EDUCATION:	Maryvale uses 18 different public and parochial schools in its own and neighboring communities. Children are enrolled in school program best suited to individual needs. There is an on-grounds junior high school class (ESEA) with a capacity of 10 and two senior high Educationally Handicapped classes with a capacity of 12. Tutoring through the Special Learning Center on-grounds is available to all.
TREATMENT:	Girls live in groups of 15, in apartment-like structures, located on 14 acres of land. Senior housemothers live on grounds and are assisted by non-resident housemothers. Treatment team approach is utilized with social worker, house-

parents, psychiatrist, and psychologist. The
living group seen as a treatment unit. There is
group therapy, and each child seen individually
at least once per week by a social worker. Family
counseling is also available.

RECREATION: Special transportation is provided for girls parti-
cipating in extracurricular activities. There is
an on-grounds gym-auditorium, a swimming
pool, playground equipment, and park. A camp
program operates during summer vacation.

7/74

FACT SHEET

Name: MARYVALE
Address: 7600 E. Graves Avenue, Rosemead, CA. 91770
Telephone: (213) 280-6510
Licensed by: California State Department of Health
Auspices: Private
Age Range: Girls - 3 through 18
                    Boys - 3 through 11
Administrator: Sister Mary Elizabeth, ACSW
Social Service
  Supervisor: James G. Hansen, ACSW

1. Treatment
    To provide an atmosphere or milieu through which the child can develop
and grow physically, mentally, emotionally, socially, educationally, and
spiritually. Placement is usually seen as a temporary necessity, affording
time during which the child can resolve personal or behavioral problems or
problems with or within his/her family.

2. Method
    The greatest emphasis is upon group living. Maryvale has six living
groups with up to 14 children in a group. Under adult supervision and through
day-to-day living, the child is helped to grow and mature. The child is
further aided in regular group meetings through sharing of feelings and
experiences, and confrontation of undesirable behavior. These meetings
within the group range from one to five per week.

3. Staff Function
    A. Houseparents. Houseparents provide the necessary daily adult
        supervision, care, and nourishments, and participate in group
        meetings.
    B. Social Workers. Each group of children has its own social worker
        who provides casework and counseling services to the child and
        family. The social worker is a co-leader in group meetings.
    C. Psychiatrist/Psychologist. Psychiatric/psychological doctor
        consultants provide evaluation, counseling, consultation, group
        therapy, and in-service training sessions.

4. Educational Opportunities

    Maryvale utilizes 16 public and parochial elementary and high schools
in this area. Maryvale provides the busing of children to and from school.
The variety of schools enables Maryvale to place a child in the school which

will best meet his/her needs. Maryvale has five on-grounds special classes (EH) for grades 1-3, 5-8, and 9-12. These programs are for children of average or better intelligence who are having difficulty in learning. We do not have special facilities for the mentally retarded.

5.   Program
    Each living group has three to four houseparents and a Sister Supervisor. Each group has a full-time social worker and a one-day a week doctor consultant (psychologist or psychiatrist). The sleeping quarters are small dormitories (five to a dorm) and adjacent are television room, recreation room and a group dining room/kitchen. Weekdays, dinners are provided from a central kitchen. All other meals are made in the individual group dining/kitchen area with the children/adolescents participating in the preparation. The children/adolescents are bussed to their various off-grounds schools; upon return the children/adolescents are involved in free time activity, recreation, group meetings, tutoring, employment (older girls) through to bedtime.

    Maryvale has a special learning center with programmed learning aids where younger children can be tutored and supervised by the staff and adolescent girls. The cottage for younger children (boys and girls 3-11 years) has a bilingual staff who do well with children unable to speak English. All children/adolescents are provided allowances and clothing money. The oldest handle their own money and purchase their own clothes.

    Dating is permitted on grounds, in groups, or individually, depending on the individual level of maturity. Smoking for high school girls is permitted with parental approval.

    Great effort is made to keep girls integrated into the community. Special transportation is provided for girls participating in extra-curricular activities. There is an on-grounds gym-auditorium, a swimming pool, playground equipment and park on Maryvale's 14 acres. A camp program operates during summer vacation. A mountain cabin in Crestline is available for small groups to visit on weekends.

6.   Intake Criteria
    Almost all children/adolescents with behavior problems will be given serious consideration for placement. The exceptions are the mentally retarded, physically handicapped, chronic and confirmed drug users and drug pushers. Maryvale is an open setting with much interaction for educational, recreational, social, and cultural purposes with the community. Maryvale cannot provide a closed setting if such is needed for any particular child/adolescent.

7. Referral Procedure
        A telephone call to the Social Service Department secretary at any time
during business hours will begin the process. As soon as possible, there-
after, the Director of Social Services or a staff social worker will return
your call. A determination at this point will be made as to whether or not
the Maryvale program seems appropriate for fulfilling the child's/adolescent's
needs. If so, you will be given an intake date and you will be requested, in
the meanwhile, to forward to us current school reports, social summary,
and any psychological/psychiatric reports available. At intake a final
determination will be made as to whether Maryvale is the placement of choice
for the child. If it is, a preplacement or placement date will be set up.

5/1/75

Appendix IV

Item comparison on selected test questions:

Question 3: Those who get the best jobs are usually the ones who--

1) know the right person; 2) are the best trained; 3) are the luckiest; 4) work

the hardest.

Group	Percent Answer #1	Percent Answer #2	Percent Answer #3	Percent Answer #4
600-boys N=13	7.7	38.5	7.7	46.2
600-girls N=19		47.4	5.3	47.4
601-boys N=3	33.3	33.3		33.3
601-girls N=11		63.6	36.4	
602-boys N=20	15.0	35.0	5.0	45.0
602-girls N=26	19.2	38.5	7.7	24.6
Maryvale N=40	5.0	60.0	5.0	30.0
Pacific Lodge N=40	5.0	45.0	5.0	45.0
High School-Boys N=40	17.5	55.0	5.0	22.5
High School-Girls N=43	9.3	46.5	11.6	32.6

Question 5: If a person called me a dirty name, I would--

1) fight the person; 2) tell him where to get off; 3) say and do nothing; 4) laugh

it off.

Group	Percent Answer #1	Percent Answer #2	Percent Answer #3	Percent Answer #4
600-boys N=13	7.7	30.8	46.2	15.4
600-girls N=19	10.5	21.1	31.6	36.8
601-boys N=3	33.3	33.3	33.3	
601-girls N=11	9.1	36.4	27.3	27.3
602-boys N=21	19.0	33.3	28.6	19.0
602-girls N=26	23.1	30.8	7.7	38.5
Pacific Lodge N=41	7.3	53.7	19.5	19.5
Maryvale N=40	7.5	57.5	20.0	15.0
High School-boys N=37	8.1	37.8	16.2	37.8
High School-girls N=44	15.9	34.1	29.5	20.5

Question 8: Parents usually understand their children:

1) very well; 2) quite well; 3) not very well; 4) not at all.

Group	Percent Answer #1	Percent Answer #2	Percent Answer #3	Percent Answer #4
600-boys N=13	23.1	15.4	46.2	15.4
600-girls N=19	21.1	36.8	42.1	
601-boys N=3		33.3	66.7	
601-girls N=11	18.2		72.7	9.1
602-boys N=19	42.1	10.5	42.1	5.3
602-girls N=26	23.1	30.8	38.5	
Maryvale N=40	7.5	17.5	60.0	15.0
Pacific Lodge N=40	12.5	27.5	52.5	7.5
High School-boys N=39	20.5	30.8	43.6	5.1
High School-girls N=44	18.2	25.0	43.2	13.6

Question 23: The school work that the teacher gives me is usually;

1) very hard; 2) fairly hard; 3) fairly easy; 4) very easy.

Group	Percent Answer #1	Percent Answer #2	Percent Answer #3	Percent Answer #4
600-boys N=13	8.3	58.3	25.0	8.3
600-girls N=19	6.3	50.0	37.5	6.3
601-boys N=3	33.3		66.7	
601-girls N=10		20.0	60.0	20.0
602-boys N=21	19.0	42.9	19.0	19.0
602-girls N=24	12.5	33.3	54.2	
Maryvale N=41	9.8	36.6	46.3	7.3
Pacific Lodge N=41	2.6	68.4	21.1	7.9
High School-boys N=40	2.5	45.0	50.0	2.5
High School-girls N=44	15.9	34.1	29.5	20.5

Question 27: Most policemen try to--

1) help you; 2) scare you; 3) boss you; 4) get something on you.

Group	Percent Answer #1	Percent Answer #2	Percent Answer #3	Percent Answer #4
600-boys N=12	33.3	8.3	16.7	41.7
600-girls N=17	47.1	11.8	17.6	23.5
601-boys N=3		33.3	66.7	
601-girls N=11	18.2	9.1	45.5	27.3
602-boys N=20	35.0	15.0	15.0	35.0
602-girls N=25	24.0	8.0	16.0	52.0
Maryvale N=41	39.0	14.6	26.8	19.5
Pacific Lodge N=41	56.1	4.9	9.8	29.3
High School-boys N=40	56.4	10.3	15.4	17.9
High School-girls N=44	59.1	20.5	6.8	13.6

Question 29: Cheating in school is usually done by--

1) only a few bad pupils; 2) none of the pupils; 3) most of the pupils 4) all of the pupils.

Group	Percent Answer #1	Percent Answer #2	Percent Answer #3	Percent Answer #4
600-boys N=12	66.7		25.0	8.3
600-girls N=17	52.9		47.1	
601-boys N=3	33.3	33.3		33.3
601-girls N=11	36.4	18.2	36.4	9.1
602-boys N=20	55.0	15.0	20.0	10.0
602-girls N=26	42.3	3.8	30.8	23.1
Maryvale N=40	50.0		42.5	7.5
Pacific Lodge N=39	56.4	7.7	30.8	5.1
High School-boys N=40	42.5	5.0	42.5	10.0
High School-girls N=44	34.1	9.1	40.9	15.9

Question 38: When I leave school or graduate, I will--

1) take any job that comes along; 2) find a good job; 3) take it easy for awhile;

4) go to another school or college.

Group	Percent Answer #1	Percent Answer #2	Percent Answer #3	Percent Answer #4
600-boys N=12	8.3	41.7	16.7	33.3
600-girls N=15		46.7	6.7	46.7
601-boys N=3		66.7	33.3	
601-girls N=11	9.1	72.7	18.2	
602-boys N=20	25.0	40.0	15.0	20.0
602-girls N=25	11.5	38.5	15.4	30.8
Maryvale N=41		51.2	9.8	39.0
Pacific Lodge N=41	12.2	41.5	9.8	36.6
High School-boys N=39	7.7	30.8	10.3	51.3
High School-girls N=44		22.7	13.6	63.6

Question 42: For the most serious trouble I have ever been in--

1) others were to blame more than I was; 2) others were to blame as much as I was;

3) I was mostly to blame; 4) I was wholly to blame.

Group	Percent Answer #1	Percent Answer #2	Percent Answer #3	Percent Answer #4
600-boys N=13	15.4	30.8	38.5	15.4
600-girls N=18	20.0	26.7	40.0	13.3
601-boys N=3		66.7	33.3	
601-girls N=11		54.5	18.2	27.3
602-boys N=18	16.7	16.7	38.9	27.8
602-girls N=25	12.0	24.0	40.0	24.0
Maryvale N=41	4.9	48.8	24.4	22.0

Question 42 (Continued)

Pacific Lodge N=40	12.5	17.5	45.0	25.0
High School-boys N=37	24.3	35.1	18.9	21.6
High School-girls N=44	27.3	40.9	20.5	11.4

Question 52: I have been--

1) extremely lucky; 2) lucky; 3) extremely unlucky; 4) unlucky.

Group	Percent Answer #1	Percent Answer #2	Percent Answer #3	Percent Answer #4
600-boys N=12	8.3	41.7	25.0	25.0
600-girls N=16	18.8	18.8	31.3	31.3
601-boys N=2			100	
601-girls N=11	9.1	27.3	45.5	18.2
602-boys N=20	10.0	45.0	25.0	20.0
602-girls N=25	15.4	15.4	30.8	38.4
Maryvale N=41	4.9	61.0	19.5	14.6
Pacific Lodge N=39	23.1	41.0	17.9	17.9
High School-boys N=38	7.9	73.7	17.9	17.9
High School-girls N=44	6.8	65.9	9.1	18.2

Question 63: The Police--

1) are usually very fair; 2) make some mistakes; 3) favor the rich; 4) are usually

unfair.

Group	Percent Answer #1	Percent Answer #2	Percent Answer #3	Percent Answer #4
600-boys N=12	25.0	8.3	8.3	58.3
600-girls N=15	20.0	20.0	6.7	53.3
601-boys N=2				100
601-girls N=11		45.5	9.1	45.5
602-boys N=17	12.5	31.3	25.0	31.3
602-girls N=26	7.7	26.9	26.9	38.4
Maryvale N=41	17.1	43.9	4.9	34.1
Pacific Lodge N=40	10.0	45.0	5.0	40.0
High School-boys N=37	16.2	59.5	2.7	21.6
High School-girls N=43	9.3	46.5	11.6	32.6

BIBLIOGRAPHY BOOKS

1. Adams, Gary B., et al. Juvenile Justice Management. Charles C. Thomas, Springfield, no date.

2. Brieland, Donald, Costin, Lela B., and Atherton, Charles R. Contemporary Social Work. McGraw Hill Book Co., New York, 1975.

3. Cloward, Richard A. and Ohlin, Lloyd. Delinquency and Opportunity, A Theory of Delinquent Gangs. Free Press of Glencoe, 1960.

4. Cohen, Albert K. Delinquent Boys, The Culture of the Gang. The Free Press, Glencoe, Ill., 1955.

5. Danzin, Norman K., Ed. Children and Their Caretakers. Transaction Books, New Jersey, 1973.

6. Frederickson, Hazel and Mulligan, R. A. The Child and His Welfare. W. H. Freeman and Co., San Francisco, 1972.

7. Glueck, Sheldon and Glueck, Eleanor. Predicting Delinquency and Crime. Harvard University Press, Cambridge, 1958.

8. Glueck, Sheldon and Glueck, Eleanor. Delinquents in the Making, Paths to Prevention. Harper and Brothers, New York, 1952.

9. Goldstein, Joseph, Freud, Anna, and Solnit, Albert J. Beyond the Best Interests of the Child. The Free Press, New York, 1973.

10. Haskell, Martin R. and Yablonsky, Lewis. Juvenile Delinquency. Rand, McNally College Publishing Co., Chicago, 1974.

11. Henry, Nelson, B., Ed. 47th Yearbook of the National Society for the Study of Education, Part I, Delinquency and the Schools. University of Chicago Press, 1948.

12. James, Howard. Children in Trouble: A National Scandal. David McKay Co., Inc., New York, 1969.

13. Kassebaum, Gene. Delinquency and Social Policy. Prentiss-Hall, Inc., New Jersey, 1974.

14. Katz, Sanford W., Ed. The Youngest Minority. American Bar Association, 1974.

15. Klein, Malcolm W. *Street Gangs and Street Workers*. Prentice-Hall, Inc., Englewood Cliffs, New Jersey, 1971.

16. Kvaraceus, William C. *The Community and the Delinquent*. World Book Co., 1954.

17. Kvaraceus, William C. *Anxious Youth: Dynamics of Delinquency*. Charles E. Merrill Books, Inc., Mass., 1966.

18. Lerman, Paul. *Delinquency and Social Policy*. Praeger Publishers, New York, 1970.

19. Levine, Abraham. The Seventh Step Foundation: Differential Association and a Peer Self Help Group. Unpublished Master's Thesis, California State University, Los Angeles, 1970.

20. Ramsey, Charles E. *Problems of Youth*. Dickenson Publishing Co., Belmont, California, 1967.

21. Shaw, Clifford R., and McKay, Henry D. *Juvenile Delinquency and Urban Areas*. University of Chicago Press, Chicago, 1942, Rev. 1969.

22. Tait, C. Downing Jr., MD, and Hodges, Emory F. Jr. MD. *Delinquents, Their Families and The Community*. Charles C. Thomas, Illnois, 1962.

23. Tunley, Roul. *Kids, Crime and Chaos*. Dell Publishing Co., Inc., New York, 1962.

24. Wolfanger, Marvin E., Savitz, Leonard and Johnston, Norman, Eds. *The Sociology of Crime and Delinquency*. John Wiley and Sons, Inc.,

BIBLIOGRAPHY PERIODICALS

1. Balogh, Joseph K. "Juvenile Delinquency Proneness: A Study of Predictive Factors Involved in Delinquent Phenomena." Juvenile Criminal Law, 1958. Number 48. pp. 615-618.

2. Boyarsky, Nancy. "Dilemma of the Out-of-Control Child." Los Angeles Times, 5/18/75.

3. Canary, Peyton. "Program Gives Youth Offenders a Second Chance," Los Angeles Times, 7/6/75.

4. Children's Services Advisory Committee, "Position Statement of Los Angeles County DPSS Children's Services Staff Re Juvenile Court Dependency Program, June, 1974.

5. Escalante, Alicia, Welfare Right Organization, Statement before Los Angeles County Public Social Services Commission, May, 1974.

6. Feldhusen, John F., Brenning, James J. and Thruston, John R., Purdue University, "Prediction of Delinquency, Adjustment and Academic Achievement over a Five Year Period with the KD Proneness Scale," Journal of Educational Research, April 1972, Volume 65 (8), pp. 375-381.

7. Follman, John, et al. (University of South Florida), "Delinquency Prediction Scales and Personality Inventories," Child Study Journal.

8. Gillespie, Mary. Statement before Los Angeles County Public Social Services Commission, May, 1974.

9. Knight, Doug, "Second Thoughts," Human Behavior, December 1975, pp. 9-10.

10. Kvaraceus, William C. Delinquency Behavior 1959, National Education Association, Washington D.C.

11. Kvaraceus, William C. "Prediction Studies of Delinquent Behavior," Personnel and Guidance Journal, November, 1955, pp. 147-149.

12. Murphy, Ellis P. Statement to Los Angeles County Supervisor Hayes, Public Hearings on Juvenile Justice, January 1974.

13. Steele, Brandt F. "Working with Abusive Parents: A Psychiatrist's View, Children Today, Volume 4, p. 3, May and June, 1975.

14. Thomas, Ivory J. The Juvenile Homicide Suspect and the Juvenile System. Unpublished Master's Thesis, Pepperdine University, 1975.

15. State of California, Welfare and Institutions Code, Laws Relating to Youthful Offenders.

16. Wakelin, Diane. Hamburger Home, Statement before Los Angeles County Public Social Services Commission, May, 1974.

17. Zeman, Ray. "Juvenile Arrests for Murder up in County," Los Angeles Times, 11/4/75.

18. Kumbula, Tendayi. "Juvenile Justice Inequities Assailed," Los Angeles Times, 5/4/75.

19. Footlick, Jerrold K. "Children and the Law," Newsweek Magazine, 9/8/75.

20. Dallinger, R W. "Juvenile Justice, Kids or Society," Los Angeles Free Press, Volume 12, #46 (591) November 14-20, 1975.

GOVERNMENT PUBLICATIONS

1. *California Laws Relating to Youthful Offenders*, Department of the Youth Authority of the State of California, 1972.

2. National Advisory Commission on Criminal Justice Standards and Goals, *A National Strategy to Reduce Crime*, U.S. Government Printing Office, 1973.

3. The President's Commission on Law Enforcement and Administration of Justice, *The Challenge of Crime in a Free Society*, U.S. Government Printing Office, 1967.

4. *Task Force Report: Juvenile Delinquency and Youth Crime*, Report on Juvenile Justice and Consultants' Papers, Task Force on Juvenile Delinquency. The President's Commission on Law Enforcement and Administration of Justice, 1967.

NOTES

1. FBI Uniform Crime Reports listing of the Index Crimes:

   Willful Homicide, Forcible Rape, Robbery, Aggravated
   Assault, Burglary, Larceny $50 and over, Motor Vehicle
   Theft.

2. Statistics represent figures from Los Angeles County Probation Department (see Appendix) Los Angeles County Public
   Social Services Commission.

3. It should be noted that minor offenders are <u>not</u> sent to Youth
   Authority facilities.

4. Summaries from Klein, Malcolm W., <u>Street Gangs and Street
   Workers</u>, Prentice-Hall Inc., Englewood Cliffs, New Jersey,
   1971, pp. 26-38.